This book
belongs to:

_____

_____

My Own Little Promise Bible

Copyright © 2019 by Christian Art Kids, an imprint of Christian Art Publishers, PO Box 1599, Vereeniging, 1930, RSA

© 2019
First edition 2019

Cover designed by Christian Art Kids
Designed by Christian Art Kids

Images used under license from Shutterstock.com
Illustrations by Marlaine Michie

Scripture quotations are taken from the *Holy Bible,* New Living Translation®, copyright © 1996, 2004, 2007, 2013, 2015 by Tyndale House Foundation. Used by permission of Tyndale House Publishers, Inc., Carol Stream, Illinois 60188. All rights reserved.

Scripture quotations are taken from the *Holy Bible*, New International Version® NIV®. Copyright © 1973, 1978, 1984, 2011 by International Bible Society. Used by permission of Biblica, Inc.® All rights reserved worldwide.

Scripture quotations are taken from the *Holy Bible*, GOD'S WORD Translation. Copyright © 1995 by God's Word to the Nations. Used by permission of Baker Publishing Group. All rights reserved.

Scripture quotations are taken from the *Holy Bible,* Good News Translation® (Today's English Version, Second Edition). Copyright © 1992 by American Bible Society. All rights reserved.

Printed in China

ISBN 978-1-4321-2487-8

19 20 21 22 23 24 25 26 27 28 – 10 9 8 7 6 5 4 3 2 1

Printed in Shenzhen, China
November 2018
Print Run: 100409

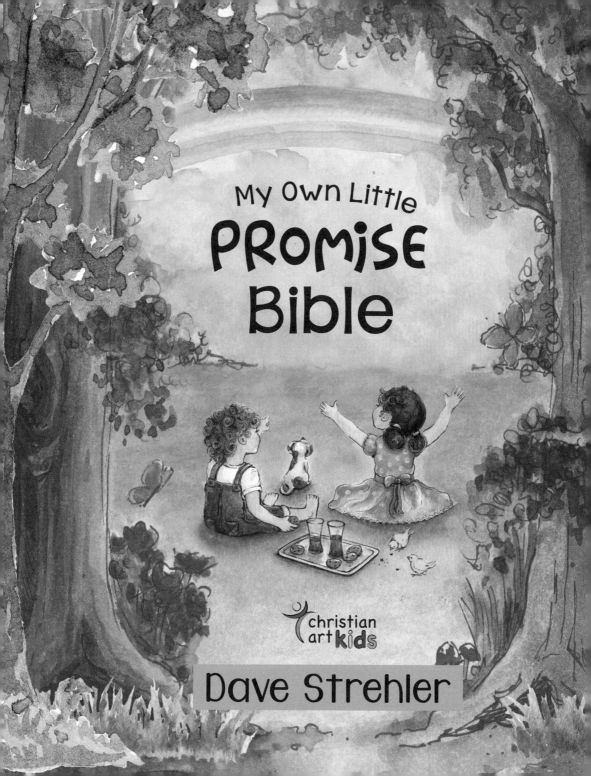

My Own Little
PROMISE
Bible

christian
art kids

Dave Strehler

Contents

To

Logan and Harper.
May you shine like stars
in the world as you learn to love
and trust God from an early age.

(SEE PHILIPPIANS 2:13-15)

God's Promises

Whenever God says
that He will do something
or that something will happen,
it is a promise.

When God speaks, it is done!

In the Beginning, God Spoke

Before time began, there was nothing – no sun, no moon, no stars. There were no birds, no fish, no bears. And, of course, there were no people.

Everything was dark; everything was quiet!

Then God decided to create a very beautiful place – a place where people could enjoy all He had made.

So God spoke.

His powerful words put stars where they should be and hung the moon in the sky. His words made grass cover the hills and flowers speckle the fields. God's words made the fruit trees grow and caused the streams to flow. His powerful words brought life to every creature on earth, big and small.

Then God created people. And God loved the people He had made. He loved them so much that He wanted to talk to them. He wanted to tell them what He is like and what pleases Him. He also wanted to tell them about the plans He had for them.

But sadly, most of the people didn't follow God's ways and they didn't listen to Him. How would they ever know about the wonderful things God wanted to do for them?

Read: Psalm 33:6

The good thing is, among the people were some who did love God. They listened to Him and obeyed Him. So God spoke to them. He told them what to say to the others.

God promised to forgive people for their sins and to care for them. For those who obeyed Him, God would do everything He had promised.

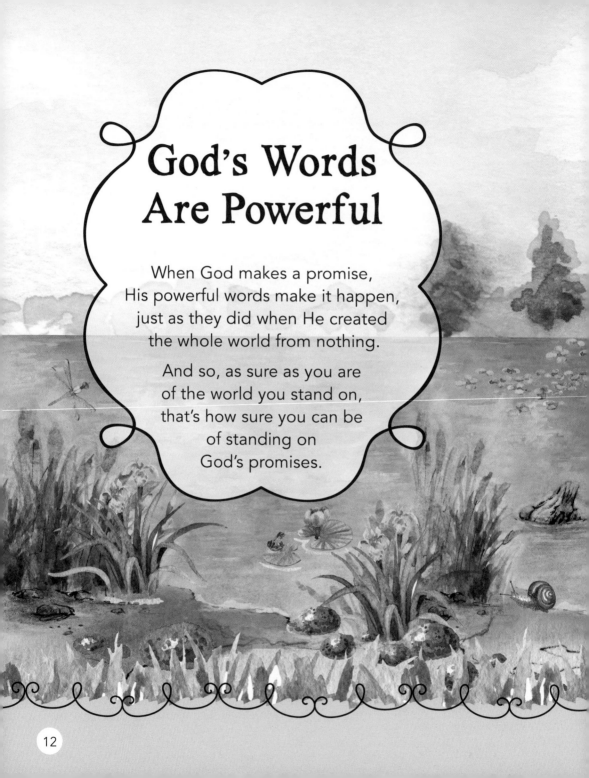

God's Words Are Powerful

When God makes a promise, His powerful words make it happen, just as they did when He created the whole world from nothing.

And so, as sure as you are of the world you stand on, that's how sure you can be of standing on God's promises.

God is able to make
every promise come true!

Promises
in the Bible

God's wonderful promises are just waiting to be discovered by you. And although trying to find them in the Bible might seem like a frightening task, they're actually real easy to find once you know where to look.

In the Old Testament, God's promises can be found in three main areas:

- There are powerful promises woven into the life-stories of people who trusted God.

- You will find precious promises of God's care in the beautiful words of the Psalms.

- Some promises are like treasure buried under the ruins of an old city. These promises of hope can be found when digging through the messages of the prophets.

In the New Testament, God's promises can be found in two main areas:

- Jesus shared comforting promises with His followers as He taught them life-changing Truths.
- You will also discover exciting promises in the letters that godly leaders wrote to encourage new believers.

This means that the whole Bible is full of God's promises. Each promise is a precious treasure to those who believe that God is able do all that He said He would.

Why Has God Given Us so Many Promises?

Faith • Hope • Love

God Wants Us to Trust Him

Faith

When we fully trust God to do what He has said, we please God and our faith in Him grows.

We please God
when we expect Him to do something.
And we please God
when we believe that He is able to do it.

Faith is knowing, for sure, that what we hope for will actually happen. Faith helps us to believe in things we cannot see.

(SEE HEBREWS 11:1)

And when we do see God working out a promise in our lives, we learn to trust Him even more!

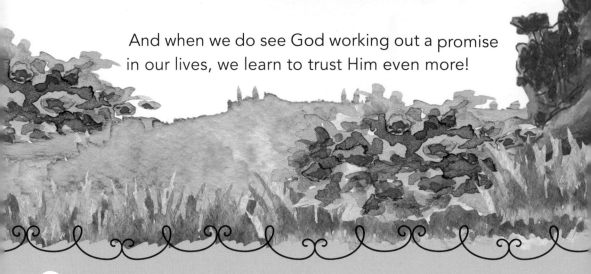

By faith we can say ...

I believe

that God will take care of me
because
He promises to keep us safe. His Word says,

The LORD will keep you from all harm –
He will watch over your life.

PSALM 121:7

By faith we can say ...

I believe

that God will give me what I need
because
Jesus promises that His heavenly Father
will look after us
just as He feeds little birds, and
He will make sure we have clothes
just as He makes petals for flowers.

(SEE MATTHEW 6:26, 30)

God Wants Us to Know His Plan

Hope

Did you know that God has a very special plan for your life? He loved you and thought about your life before you were even born.

> Before you were a day old,
> every day of your life
> was written in His big book.
>
> (SEE PSALM 139:16)

God can see into the future. He knows what will happen tomorrow, next Friday, and at your next birthday.

God has worked out a special plan for your life with exciting things that no one knows about. And because no one knows God's secret plan, no one can change His plan for your life! So, even when things don't seem to be going right, you can look up and thank God that He's got everything worked out.

We have a wonderful promise from God – a promise of hope:

God said, "I know the plans I have for you.
I have planned good things for you;
not things that will harm you.
I have plans that will give you
hope for the days to come."

(SEE JEREMIAH 29:11)

That means ...

You don't have to worry about what will happen in the future. God is excited to share His plan with you, little by little. He will show you the way to go, a step at a time, and keep you on the right path.

God's plan gives me hope.

God Wants Us to Feel Loved
Love

God loves us more than we can ever imagine. He talks to us through His Word, the Bible, where He tells us about His love.

In His Word, He gives us promises and makes them real in our lives so that we learn to trust His love.

> God is a faithful God who keeps His promises
> and shows His love to those who
> love Him and obey His commands.
>
> (SEE DEUTERONOMY 7:9)

God's promise of a calming love shows how excited He gets about us. He said to His people,

> The LORD your God is living among you ...
> He will take delight in you with gladness.
> With His love, He will calm all your fears.
> He will rejoice over you with joyful songs.
>
> ZEPHANIAH 3:17

Then God sent Jesus to show us His love. Jesus became a man and lived among us. He loved us so much that He died to save us from sin so we can live with Him forever.

But Jesus didn't stay dead. After three days He was made alive again by God's power!

Jesus then made a promise before He went back to heaven. He promised to send the Holy Spirit to be with us and comfort us with His love.

The Holy Spirit now lives in the hearts of all those who believe in God. So now, God is with us all the time. And when we feel His closeness and love, He calms our troubled hearts.

Read: Isaiah 7:14, John 3:16, John 14:16, Romans 5:5

Promises That Show Us What God Is Like

The more we get to know God,
the more we will want to worship Him
for who He is and for what He has done.

God Is Mighty
He is powerful

As we look around us, we get a little peek of how powerful God is.

His power may be quiet, like when He makes the sun come up. His power may go unnoticed, like when He slowly changes the seasons right around the world.

But when we hear of powerful tornadoes and exploding volcanoes, we realize how powerful God's hands are. He made the deep sea and shaped the dry land with His hands. And now His invisible hands keep everything in place.

God holds us in the palm
of His hand and no one
can take us away from Him.

(SEE JOHN 10:27-29)

Read: Psalm 95:5, Psalm 119:73, Colossians 1:17

Lord,

I am amazed by Your great power. Your hands put the world in its place and Your hands made me. You get the sun up every morning and in the evening You let it go down again. When it is dark, Your mighty hand moves the moon across the night sky, and with that same mighty hand You hold me safe.

Amen

God Is Eternal
He has no beginning and no end

Some years ago, on a very special day, you came into the world. That was the day you were born. And now, every time it's your birthday, you are a whole year older!

But God had no beginning. Imagine that. He just was! That's why God calls Himself "I AM." God just is and He will always be. That's one thing we can know for sure.

> For the LORD is good. His unfailing love
> continues forever, and His faithfulness
> continues to each generation.
>
> PSALM 100:5

A generation is a group of people who grew up together at about the same time. Your grandparents are one generation. Your parents are the next generation, and you are part of the new generation.

God promises that from one generation to the next, He carries on being there for each one, and to be faithful to His promises.

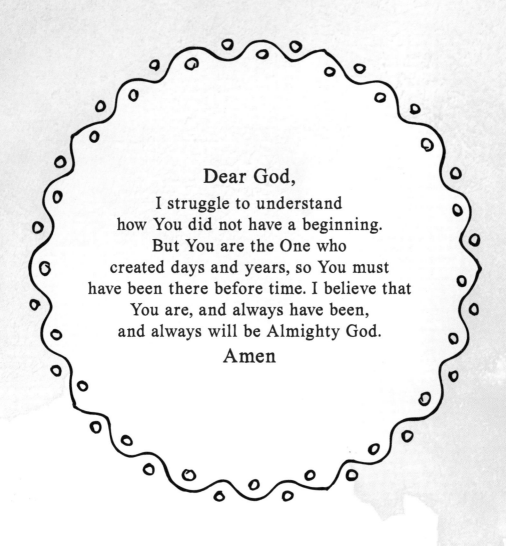

Dear God,

I struggle to understand
how You did not have a beginning.
But You are the One who
created days and years, so You must
have been there before time. I believe that
You are, and always have been,
and always will be Almighty God.

Amen

God Is Faithful

He will never leave you

When God wants us to do something, He will always help us to do it. He will never leave us to struggle on our own.

God wants us to *become part* of His kingdom, and
God wants us to *work* in His kingdom.

We become part of God's kingdom the moment we ask Him to forgive us and make us new. He takes us into His family and then helps us to become more and more like Him.

> God will make this happen,
> for He who calls you is faithful.
>
> 1 THESSALONIANS 5:24

God will help us to do the tasks He has planned for us. He wants us to pray for others, help others, and tell others all about Him.

Read: Psalm 47:7

Dear heavenly Father,
Thank You that You are helping me to want to do the things that please You. You are the faithful God who will make this happen.
Amen

For God is working in you, giving you the desire and the power to do what pleases Him.

PHILIPPIANS 2:13

God Is Unchanging
He is always the same

Everything around us is changing. Some things change really slowly. Some things change in a flash. You are changing. Others are changing.

Some change their minds about what they've said. Some make promises they don't plan to keep. But ...

> God is not a man, so He does not lie.
> He is not human, so He does not change His mind.
> Has He ever spoken and failed to act?
> Has He ever promised and not carried it through?
>
> NUMBERS 23:19

We all have our ups and downs. Sometimes we feel like doing things, and sometimes we're too tired. Sometimes we like our friends a lot, and sometimes we don't. Sometimes we remember, and sometimes we forget.

But God never forgets His promises. He never makes a promise He doesn't plan to keep. And God won't suddenly change His mind about His promises when we've disappointed Him.

God keeps His promises, no matter what!

Lord God,

Thank You that I can always depend on You and trust You. You are a God who is always the same. You are always kind and good.

Amen

God Is Patient

He gently helps us grow in our faith

Jesus promised to come back and take us to heaven to be with Him. But until that day, God is working in the heart of each one of us. He has left us here on earth for a while so that our faith has a chance to grow, and that others can get to know Him too.

> The Lord isn't really being slow about His promise, as some people think. No, He is being patient for your sake.
>
> 2 PETER 3:9

God is making our hearts beautiful. He wants others to see our kindness, humility and gentleness. And so, God is waiting for people to be ready for that great day when Jesus comes back.

God waits patiently for us and helps us to grow.

Read: John 14:2-3, Colossians 3:12

Lord,
I praise You that You are so patient. Even when I slip up and do wrong, You are willing to forgive me and help me to try again. Thank You, Lord, that You are helping me to become more like You.

Amen

God Is Everywhere

He is with us wherever we are

Although God is in heaven, He is also with us here on earth. God watches over us, wherever we are and wherever we go. There is no place on earth, or even in space, where He cannot see us.

A man named Jonah foolishly tried to run away from God. He hid in the bottom of a ship. But God knew where he was. Jonah found out that God sees us wherever we are. And that's a good thing, because God is the One who looks after us and protects us.

Because God is everywhere, no matter where we go, God is already there to guide and help us.

If I climb upward on the rays of
the morning sun or land on the most distant shore
of the sea where the sun sets, even there Your
hand would guide me and Your
right hand would hold on to me.

PSALM 139:9-10

Read: Isaiah 57:15, Jonah 1

Heavenly Lord,
You are the mighty God who rules
from Your throne! But You don't just
watch me from heaven,
You hold on to me, and Your powerful
hand gently leads me through life.
Amen

God Is Merciful

He gives and forgives

Mercy means forgiving and being kind to someone who has wronged us. Mercy can also mean helping someone who is weak or in need.

Every one of us has sinned against God. We don't deserve to be forgiven, but God loves us and longs to forgive us.

> If we confess our sins,
> He forgives them and cleanses us
> from everything we've done wrong.
>
> 1 JOHN 1:9

Our sin is like a dark cloud that hides us from God. God wants to take our sin away so that He can see us and enjoy us. Once we have decided to follow after God, He wants to keep our hearts clean because that is where His Spirit lives.

To have a clean heart, you need to ask God to forgive you, just like when you say sorry to someone.

42   Read: Psalm 41:4, Luke 18:35-42, Psalm 103:8-10, Isaiah 59:2

Lord,

Please forgive me and make my heart clean. Help me, Lord, to do what is right and good so that I will please You.

Amen

God Is Righteous
He is pure and good

God can do what He has promised because He is all-powerful, and nothing can stop Him!

God *will* do what He has promised because He is righteous and true.

But God also *wants* to do what He has promised. He is good to all and longs to bless us.

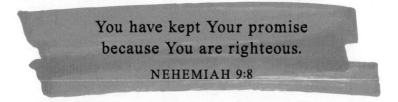

You have kept Your promise
because You are righteous.

NEHEMIAH 9:8

God is righteous, which means He is completely good. And because God is good, everything He does is good. He has promised to share His *eternal* nature with us so that we can live forever, just as He lives forever.

He has also promised to share His *perfect* nature with us. Here on earth, God is helping us to become more and more like Him. And one day, when we are in heaven, He will make us perfectly good, just as He is good.

Read: Psalm 145:17, 2 Corinthians 3:18, 1 John 3:2

Because of His glory and excellence,
He has given us great and precious promises.
These are the promises that enable you to
share His divine nature ...

2 PETER 1:4

Lord,

All that is good comes from You. Thank You for
Your promise that, one day when I see You, I will
be perfect.

Amen

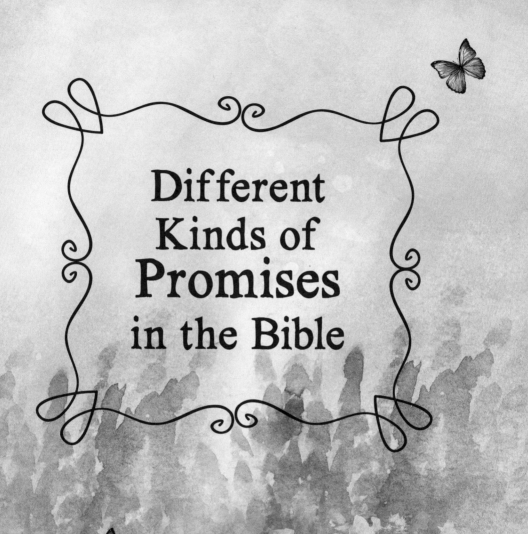

Different Kinds of Promises in the Bible

A General Promise

A promise for everyone

General promises are like a big, invisible blanket of blessing that covers all people for all time. These promises are for everyone – even for those who don't believe in God.

God loves every single person He created. He has given us promises that show His kindness to all. One of these promises is in the story of Noah, where God made a promise to all people.

In Noah's time, people became so bad that they made the world a terrible place to live in. Only Noah listened to God and obeyed Him. So God told Noah to build a big boat. Then He sent a flood that covered the whole world. But Noah, his family and a whole lot of animals were kept safe in the boat.

When the flood was over, it was as though the earth had been washed clean of all the wickedness. Everything was beautiful and good. Then God made a rainbow appear in the sky, and said,

> "Whenever I form clouds over the earth, a rainbow will appear in the clouds. Then I will remember My promise to you and every living animal. Never again will water become a flood to destroy all life."
>
> GENESIS 9:14-15

God's promises will
never, ever change!

A Special Promise

A promise for certain people

In Bible times, God would sometimes make a promise to a certain person, or to a group of people. These promises are now a part of God's Word.

Today, God speaks to us through the Bible, which never changes. This means that instead of God making new promises all the time, He uses promises that are already in the Bible.

At times, as we read about God's promise to someone in the Bible, it may be that God is speaking those words to *our* hearts. When God speaks to us, we should pray about what He is telling us, and trust His Word.

God used Paul to tell many people about Jesus. Yet Paul was just an ordinary man. Like many of us, he struggled with a problem that seemed to hold him back. It felt like a thorn sticking into him. So he asked the Lord to take his problem away. But instead of making Paul's life easier, God said to him,

> "My grace is all you need.
> My power works best in weakness."
>
> 2 CORINTHIANS 12:9

Later on, Paul realized that his struggle was actually helping him. Somehow his problem made it easier for him to be humble. Instead of boasting about all the things *he* could do, Paul learned to rely on the strength that God gave him.

This promise of God's grace has encouraged many believers to trust in God's power. You, too, can ask God to help you with your weakness.

> **God's grace is more than enough for any problem.**

An "If" Promise

A promise for those who obey

There are some promises that depend on whether we obey God or not. These promises usually start with an *if*. God will do what He promised *if* we obey Him.

Long ago, the Egyptians were treating the Israelite people very badly. So the Israelites pleaded with God to rescue them, and He did. The Lord led them out of Egypt and promised them a beautiful country of their own. Then God gave them rules for living a peaceful, happy life that pleased Him. As long as they obeyed those rules, He would protect them and make sure they had enough food.

The Lord said to them,

"All these blessings will come on you and accompany you *if* you obey the LORD your God."

DEUTERONOMY 28:2

But the Israelites did not obey God. Instead, they decided to worship the evil gods of their enemies.

So God sent prophets to warn the people that He would take away His blessings. But the people didn't listen to the prophets. Then God allowed an enemy to break down their houses and take them off to a far-away land.

Because God wants to bless us, He doesn't make it difficult for us to obey Him. He will even help us to do what is right if we ask Him to. He will help us when we are weak (Hebrews 4:15-16).

Promises
That Came True
in Bible Times

Promises about Jesus

That the birth of Jesus would be a miracle

In Old Testament times, God spoke to prophets (or messengers) and told them what to say to the people. Sometimes it was a warning. Sometimes God would tell a prophet what would happen in the future. We call that a prophecy.

Some of the prophecies came true during the prophet's lifetime. Others happened much later. And some prophecies will still happen, when God's time is right.

God told Isaiah, the prophet, to let the people know that a very special baby would be born. His name would be Immanuel, which means, "God with us."

> The Lord Himself will give you this sign:
> A virgin will become pregnant and give birth
> to a Son, and she will name Him Immanuel.
>
> ISAIAH 7:14

Though many years had come and gone, God did not forget His promise. One day, He sent an angel to tell Mary that she would have a baby.

Mary wasn't married yet, so she wondered how she could have the baby. The angel told her that God would do a miracle. *He* would let her have the baby.

So God made the baby grow inside of her. That was the first miracle. The second miracle was that the baby would be a real person and God at the same time. God's promise came true and Jesus was born. God had come to earth as a man!

Read: Matthew 1:22-23

Promises about Jesus

That Jesus would be born in Bethlehem

God also gave the prophet Micah a promise about Jesus.

The One who was there when the earth was made would come to live on earth. God said,

> "But you, O Bethlehem, are only
> a small village among all the people of Judah.
> Yet a ruler of Israel, whose origins are in the
> distant past, will come from you."
>
> MICAH 5:2

Then, one day, a baby was born in the town of Bethlehem. Wise men in a far country saw a bright, new star that moved across the night sky. They decided to follow it. They walked and walked and walked. In their hearts they knew that the star could be a sign that a great king had been born.

When they reached Jerusalem, they went to ask King Herod where the special baby was. But Herod didn't know about a baby. However, he immediately called together those who knew what the prophets had written, and said to them, "Find out where God's chosen One will be born!"

Read: John 1:1-3, 2 Peter 1:19

They found the part where God had promised, "Out of Bethlehem will come a ruler who will be the Shepherd of My people."

So the wise men went on their way, and found Jesus in Bethlehem. And they worshiped Him.

Promises about Jesus
That Jesus would take away our sin

Jesus came to earth to show us what our heavenly Father is like. He showed us God's love when He came to find and save His lost sheep. In the book of Isaiah, the prophet wrote these words:

> All of us, like sheep, have strayed away.
> We have left God's paths to follow our own.
> Yet the LORD laid on Him the sins of us all.
>
> ISAIAH 53:6

God made this promise many years before Jesus came. He said that He would put all our sin on Jesus. When Jesus came and died on the cross for us, all our sin was buried with Him.

All of us are like helpless sheep. We have run away from God and gotten lost. Yet we still belong to God because He made us.

> Know that the LORD is God.
> It is He who made us, and we are His;
> we are His people, the sheep of His pasture.
>
> PSALM 100:3

Read: John 3:16, Luke 19:10, Luke 15:3-7

Although we disobeyed God, He stayed true to His promise. He sent Jesus to bring us back to Him again. And we know that the prophet was talking about Jesus taking away our sin, because Jesus said,

"I am the Good Shepherd. The Good Shepherd gives His life for the sheep."

JOHN 10:11

Promises about Jesus

That Jesus would rise again

Jesus went from place to place telling people about God and about heaven. All those who believed in Him were saved from their sin and given a new life that never ends.

Many believed in Jesus and followed Him. But others just wouldn't believe. Some hated Jesus so much that they took Him and nailed Him to a wooden cross. There on the cross, Jesus died for our sin.

Some friends of Jesus laid His body in a tomb. The bad people thought they had gotten rid of Him. However, Jesus had told His disciples that God would bring Him back to life. He knew that this Psalm was true:

> **You will not leave my soul**
> **among the dead or allow Your**
> **Holy One to rot in the grave.**
>
> **PSALM 16:10**

On the third day, an angel rolled the stone away from the tomb and Jesus came out. He was alive again, just as He had said!

Read: John 6:47, Acts 2:24-32, Colossians 1:18, Luke 24:44

This psalm of promise is about Jesus – God's Holy One – the only one who never sinned. And when Jesus takes away our sin, He makes *us* holy too!

Jesus was the first one to come back from the dead and live forever. And now, everyone who believes in Him will be made alive in their hearts and live forever too!

He is not here; He has risen, just as He said.

Promise of the Holy Spirit

That the Holy Spirit would live in us

Before Jesus came to earth, God's Spirit would come upon certain people to give them power and wisdom for a special task. The Holy Spirit brought God's power down on judges, kings and prophets. We read of God doing amazing things through Samson, David, Elijah and others.

Then one day, God said that He would send His Spirit on *everyone*! This is the promise God made:

> "I will put My Spirit in you. I will enable you to live by My laws, and you will obey My rules."
>
> EZEKIEL 36:27

Read: Judges 14:6, 1 Samuel 16:13, 1 Kings 18:46, Joel 2:28

God's plan was that Jesus would come to earth first. Jesus prepared the way for the Holy Spirit by making us clean on the inside. When we are forgiven, God through His Spirit can live inside of us.

When Jesus had finished His work on earth, He told His followers that He would send the Holy Spirit to them. The Holy Spirit would comfort them and help them to live the kind of lives that please God. Jesus said to the disciples,

> "Now I will send the Holy Spirit,
> just as My Father promised."
>
> LUKE 24:49

Then Jesus went back to heaven. Some days later, the Holy Spirit came down and filled all believers. Peter, one of the church leaders, told the people that this was what God had promised through the prophets. The Holy Spirit had come to stay.

He now lives in the hearts of all those who love God – proof that we are His children.

Promises God Makes to You

God Protects Us

Have you ever been afraid of someone? Perhaps it was someone bigger than you. Or perhaps it was a mean person who told you that something bad would happen to you.

Daniel had three friends. They had all been taken as slaves to Babylon, far from their homes. While they were in Babylon, the king decided to build a big statue. Then he ordered everyone to bow down to the statue. But Daniel's three friends worshiped only God. They said to the king, "We won't bow down and worship your gold statue!"

The king was so angry that he had the three men thrown into a very hot furnace. But nothing happened to them! Instead, there were suddenly four men in the fire because the Lord was with them.

> "Don't be afraid of the people,
> for I will be with you and will protect you.
> I, the Lord, have spoken!"
>
> JEREMIAH 1:8

When the king saw that the men were not harmed, he went up to them and ordered them to come out of the fire. The king was so amazed that God was able to save them, that he believed in God and praised Him.

Read: Daniel 3

Isn't it comforting to know that God is bigger and stronger than anyone? With God on your side, you have nothing to fear! He is with you.

Lord,
Thank You, that You are able to protect me, because You are all-powerful. And thank You that You are always with me because You love me.

Amen

God Keeps Us Safe

There are many things that can go wrong in life. All around us are things that are unsafe and even dangerous. That's why it is important to obey our parents and teachers, and keep the rules of the road.

God promises to protect His children from the dangers of everyday life.

We have fragile bodies that can easily get hurt if we are careless. That's why God has given us a warning alarm called *fear* to keep us from doing things that could hurt us.

The devil once tried to get Jesus to jump off a high building to prove that God would keep His promise.

"God says that His angels will keep you from getting hurt," the devil said, "so just jump!"

But Jesus answered, "God's Word also says that we should never do something foolish to see if God will be true to His word."

So take care. And wherever you go, God will keep His invisible wall of protection around you!

Read: Matthew 18:10, Luke 4:9-12, Psalm 34:7

He will put His angels in
charge of you to protect you
in all your ways.

PSALM 91:11

Heavenly Father,
I know that You are watching
me and looking after me all
the time. Thank You for
Your angels that protect
me from danger.

Amen

God Cares for Us

Sheep need a shepherd. They are not clever enough to find the best pasture, and they are not strong enough to protect themselves from danger.

David was a shepherd – a very good shepherd. He protected his sheep with his life. One day he wrote a psalm about God being his Shepherd and leading him to green meadows and quiet streams of water.

God is our Shepherd and we are His sheep. Isaiah the prophet wrote about how God cares *about* us and *for* us:

> He tends His flock like a shepherd:
> He gathers the lambs in His arms and
> carries them close to His heart.
>
> ISAIAH 40:11

Little lambs don't have the strength to walk far. So when the shepherd sees a lamb struggling along, he picks it up and holds it to his chest where it feels safe and warm.

The shepherd gives each sheep a name, and when he wants them to follow him, he calls them by name. God has a special name for you, and when the Holy Spirit helps you feel close to God, it's like He's giving you an invisible hug.

Read: Psalm 23:1, 1 Samuel 17:34-35, John 10:14-15, John 10:3

Dear Lord,

I feel so loved when I think of You as my Shepherd. Thank You that I am Your little sheep, and that You are my loving Shepherd.

Amen

God Protects Us from the Devil

Everything that is wrong and bad in this world begins with the devil's work in the hearts of people.

The devil is called the evil one because he hates all that is good. He tempts people to disobey God. That makes people unkind, dishonest and selfish. The devil even tries to keep those who love God from doing good.

But you don't need to fear the devil. He has no power over you because you have Jesus living in you. Jesus will protect you!

In the prayer that Jesus taught us, He asked the Father to rescue us from the evil one. When we pray that for ourselves, we are asking God to keep the devil from doing what he wants to in our lives.

> The Lord is faithful,
> and He will strengthen you
> and protect you from the evil one.
>
> 2 THESSALONIANS 3:3

Read: Colossians 1:27, Matthew 6:13, Luke 22:31-32, 2 Peter 1:3

Peter loved Jesus very much. He told Jesus that he was ready to die for Him. But later, the devil let fear fill Peter's heart when a bunch of bad people took Jesus to crucify Him.

They asked Peter whether he was a follower of Jesus. Peter replied, "No! I am not." But Jesus had prayed for Peter's faith to stay strong. And so, even though Peter had done wrong, he became a strong leader in the church. Jesus is praying for us too. When we slip up and do wrong, Jesus holds on to us so that we don't give up.

Lord Jesus,
I know I'm not perfect but I really want to please You. Help me to have the courage to do what is right.

Amen

God Hears and Answers Us

Praying is simply talking to our heavenly Father. That's what we should do all the time. Yet the Bible talks about another way of praying. When we're in big trouble, we don't just pray a normal prayer; we *call on the Lord*. It's like shouting, "Help!"

That's what Jonah did when he found himself inside a big fish. He had been thrown over the side of a ship in the middle of a storm. This all happened because he had disobeyed God and was running away.

Jonah knew he was in big trouble, and he knew that only God could help him. And so, from inside the fish, Jonah called on the Lord to rescue him. That is exactly what God wanted him to do, and that's what God wants us to do too. God says,

> "Call on Me in times of trouble.
> I will rescue you, and you will honor Me."
>
> PSALM 50:15

Read: Jonah 2:1-2, Psalm 86:7, Jeremiah 33:3, 1 Peter 3:12

God heard Jonah's cry for help even though he was under water in the stomach of a fish. It doesn't matter where you are, or what trouble you're in, God *will* hear you! Remember, God answered Jonah even though he had been disobedient. He will certainly answer your prayer for help.

When God rescues you, you'll want to tell others what He did for you, and that's how you honor Him. You also honor God when you praise Him for answering your cry for help.

Lord God,
I know that whatever trouble I'm in, You will hear me calling and You will help me.

Amen

God Guides Us

Have you ever been lost and not known which way to go? It's scary when we don't know where we are.

Using a map helps us see roads from the top, as if we were a bird flying high above. The Bible is like a map. It shows us the path God wants us to take. That's how He guides us through life. He lets us see His way so that we make good decisions.

> He guides the humble in what is right
> and teaches them His way.
>
> PSALM 25:9

One day, Abraham called his servant and said to him, "Go and find a wife for my son. God will help you."

So the servant went off. He didn't know how to decide who would be the best wife for Isaac. So he prayed to God and said, "Lord, may the woman who offers me and also my camels a drink of water be the right one."

And sure enough, while he was still praying, a woman named Rebekah came along and offered him and his camels water from the well. That's how the servant knew that she was the right wife for Isaac.

📖 Read: Psalm 119:105, Psalm 32:8, Genesis 24:1-21

When we need to make a decision and don't know what to do, we should always ask God to help us. He may use a sign to show us, like He did with Abraham's servant. But a sign can be confusing.

That's why God has given us the Bible. By reading the Bible and praying, the Holy Spirit helps our hearts to understand what God is saying to us.

If you want to do what is right, God will always show you the way!

Lord,
Thank You that You've promised to show me the way when I don't know what to do.
Amen

God Blesses Us

The Lord is always looking for a way to do favors for His children. He blesses us because He wants the very best for us. It doesn't matter if you are still small or if you haven't done anything great. He is kind and loving to all.

Before Jesus came to earth, God blessed people by letting them have many children and lots of land and animals. In some way, God's blessing could be seen by what a person had.

Job was a man with great faith and a love for God. God had blessed him with a big family and lots of animals. One terrible day, he lost everything he had. But instead of being angry, he trusted God.

So God blessed Job even more by giving him twice as much as he had before.

> The LORD remembers us and will bless us ... He will bless those who fear the LORD – small and great alike.
>
> PSALM 115:12-13

Read: Job 42:12, Matthew 5:3-10, Ephesians 1:3, Matthew 6:20

When Jesus came to earth, He told His followers that they would be blessed in a different way – with blessings that cannot be seen.

We are given new hearts where God's Spirit comes to live – wow! The Holy Spirit brings peace, joy and hope to our hearts as well as many other blessings. But that's not all. Some of our blessings are being stored up in heaven, where our treasures are safely kept for when we get there.

Dear Lord,
Even if I counted all the ways
You bless me, there would always
be one more blessing to add.
Amen

God Gives Us Wisdom

King David was getting old and it was time for his son to become the next king of Israel. David called Solomon and said to him, "Be strong and do what God wants you to do, and He will bless you."

Then David died and Solomon was made king. One night, the Lord came to Solomon in a dream, and said, "Ask for whatever you want Me to give you."

Solomon answered, "You made my father, David, a great king, but I am like a child and I don't know how to be a good king. Please give me a heart that knows right from wrong so that I can lead Your people."

The Lord was pleased that Solomon had asked for wisdom, and He gave Solomon a wise heart.

Solomon became the wisest man on earth and he wrote many proverbs. Proverbs are helpful words for living a godly life. One of the proverbs tells us where wisdom comes from:

> For the LORD gives wisdom;
> from His mouth come
> knowledge and understanding.
>
> PROVERBS 2:6

Read: 1 Kings 2:1-12, 1 Kings 3:4-15, 1 Kings 4:29

If you want to be wise, you too can ask the Lord for wisdom to know the right thing to do and say. This is the promise we have:

> If you need wisdom,
> ask our generous God,
> and He will give it to you.
>
> JAMES 1:5

Lord,
Sometimes I need to know the right thing to do. Even though I am young, please give me the wisdom to see things the way You see them.

Amen

God Gives Us All We Need

God created the universe, and so He owns it – everything there is. If you see a rock, God made it. Every tree and flower was shaped by Him. The sea and the mountains are His. Everything is His!

Because God loves you, He has promised to help you from His huge storehouse of blessing. So, when there is something you really need, remember that,

> **God will meet all your needs according to the riches of His glory in Christ Jesus.**
>
> **PHILIPPIANS 4:19**

That doesn't always mean, though, that God will give you everything you want. God has given us the ability to do certain things for ourselves. However, a time may come when we don't have what we need and there's nothing we can do about it except to trust God.

God's servant Elijah was in the desert, and there was no food to eat. But God looked after Elijah. He told the ravens to bring him bread and meat every morning and every evening.

Read: Psalm 50:9-10, Psalm 24:1, 2 Corinthians 9:8, 1 Kings 17:2-6

You may not need food or water, but you may need help in some other way. Ask God to help you.

He may help you in an unusual way, like when He used birds to feed Elijah. More often though, God will use others to help you so that they will be blessed too.

That's how God looked after Paul the missionary. Some believers had helped him when he was in need, and so Paul assured them that God would meet all their needs too.

Lord,
You know what I need right now. I believe that You can and will answer my prayer in a special way because You are faithful.

Amen

God Lifts Us Up

Sometimes our feet get in the way of each other and we stumble. Oops! Or worse, we trip over something and fall. Crash! Ouch!

Like walking along a mountain path, so our path through life has ups and downs. There are places where we easily slip and stumble. However, when we do fall, our heavenly Father helps us back on our feet. He dusts us off when it feels like no one cares.

Perhaps you did something wrong and got into trouble. Oops! Perhaps someone shouted at you and made you feel terrible on the inside. Ouch!

Everyone makes mistakes. Everyone has days when things go wrong. So when it feels like you're dirty and lying on the ground, remember this promise:

> The Lord helps the fallen and
> lifts those bent beneath their loads.
>
> PSALM 145:14

Read: James 4:10, Psalm 94:18, Psalm 37:23-24, Psalm 68:19

Perhaps you are struggling along day after day. Your heart feels heavy with sadness and your shoulders droop from being discouraged.

Look up! Jesus is there to lift that load of bad feelings and make you feel special and loved. The hope He gives will make it easy to face each new day.

Jesus said,

"Come to Me, all of you who are tired from carrying heavy loads, and I will give you rest."

MATTHEW 11:28

Jesus,

Thank You that You take the heavy load from my heart and give me Your joy to carry there instead.

Amen

God Helps Us to Be Brave

Everyone admires a hero who is brave. Being brave may mean taking the risk of getting hurt to save someone's life or defend one's country. Yet being brave doesn't mean we need to be big and strong. God says He will give us His strength!

> "Don't be afraid, for I am with you. Don't be discouraged, for I am your God. I will strengthen you and help you. I will hold you up with My victorious right hand."
>
> ISAIAH 41:10

When David was just a young shepherd boy, he rescued a lamb that was carried off by a lion. He ran after the lion, grabbed it by the hair and killed it. David risked his life to save that little lamb.

One day, David heard a giant enemy warrior mocking God and teasing the Israelite army. This made David very angry. He told King Saul that he would go to fight the giant. So David went out to meet Goliath with his sling, some stones, and God by his side. Then, with a single stone and the help of God, David conquered the giant!

Read: 1 Samuel 17, 1 Peter 5:8

Our enemy is the devil who prowls around like a lion looking for sheep. The devil causes many bad things to happen – things that hurt people and make them feel hopeless and sad. But God is our hope. He helps us in our battle against the bad things that are happening around us.

So don't be afraid or discouraged. Trust God. He will give you the power to do what is right.

Lord,

You are victorious, because You are the King of the Universe.

Amen

God Never Leaves Us

The unknown can be pretty scary – when it feels dark and we don't know what lies ahead of us. It's so much easier when the sun is shining and we can see things around us.

When we can't see at all, we need someone to hold on to – someone who *can* see. The Lord goes ahead of us all the time. When we stay close to Him, we are perfectly safe.

> The LORD is the one who is going ahead of you.
> He will be with you. He won't abandon you or leave you.
> So don't be afraid or terrified.
>
> **DEUTERONOMY 31:8**

For forty years, God led the Israelites through the desert on their way to the Promised Land. Yet He didn't just watch them from heaven. He came down to be with them as they camped along the way. And when it was time to pack up and go, the Lord went ahead of them as a cloud by day and fire by night. Not once did he get impatient with them because they were slow. He stayed with them every step of the way.

Read: Exodus 13:21-22

So when it feels dark and your heart is afraid of something that may happen, remember that God is going ahead of you. He will never, ever leave you!

Lord,
Thank You that even though I cannot see You, You are always with me.

Amen

God Keeps Us in His Peace

Fear is a strong feeling. A sudden scare can make your heart beat wildly. It can make your mind race with panicky thoughts.

Being afraid or worried all the time can make your stomach feel all tight and knotted. Perhaps that is how you are feeling right now: afraid of something that might happen in the future.

This is a promise God gave Isaiah, and a prayer we can pray:

> You will keep in perfect peace all who trust in You, all whose thoughts are fixed on You!
>
> ISAIAH 26:3

The King of Aram was very angry with the prophet Elisha and sent men to capture him. That night, they surrounded the city where Elisha was staying. Early the next morning Elisha's servant woke up to see the city surrounded by the king's army. He panicked. "Help! What are we going to do, master Elisha?" he exclaimed.

Elisha was quite calm. "Don't be afraid," he answered. Then Elisha asked the Lord to let his servant see the invisible world around him. Immediately, the servant saw a fiery army of horses and chariots that God had sent to protect them.

Read: 2 Kings 6:15-17, Philippians 4:6

Lord,

When I think of Your love and protection, my heart is peaceful and my thoughts are calm.

Amen

God Lets Us Sleep Peacefully

At the end of a long day, do you look forward to going to sleep, or do you like staying awake as long as possible?

Perhaps, while lying in bed, your busy thoughts keep going. You may imagine all sorts of bad things, or worry about the next day. However, because you live a life that pleases the Lord ...

> You can go to bed without fear;
> you will lie down and sleep soundly.
>
> **PROVERBS 3:24**

King Herod had put Peter in prison for spreading the Good News of Jesus. He was chained between two soldiers, and guards stood at the gate. Peter didn't know what they were planning to do with him. But instead of lying awake worrying, he was fast asleep.

Meanwhile, Peter's friends were praying for him. God heard their prayers and sent an angel to rescue him. A bright light shone all around Peter, but he was sleeping so soundly that the angel had to shake him. "Quick, get up and follow me," the angel said. Then the gates opened and the angel led Peter out onto the street.

Read: Acts 12:1-10, Psalm 127:2, Psalm 4:8

Lord,
Thank You that You never sleep. Instead, You are watching over me while I am sleeping.
Amen

And that's how God planned Peter's escape while he was sleeping peacefully.

In Psalms, the Lord tells us that it doesn't help to worry and scurry around. It is far better to leave everything to Him. Isn't it great that God allows His loved ones to sleep peacefully while He takes care of things?

God Forgives Us

God is holy. He is completely sinless and good. God deeply loved the people He created, but because they disobeyed Him and sinned, He could not come close to them or even look at them.

However, God had a plan. He would send His Son, Jesus, to die for us so that our sin could be taken away. And so God promised:

> "I – yes, I alone – will blot out your sins for My own sake and will never think of them again."
>
> ISAIAH 43:25

God doesn't want to keep thinking about the wrong things we've done. And so, when we ask Him to forgive us, He takes our sins so far away that He completely forgets about them – as if we had never sinned. God makes our hearts perfectly clean and puts His goodness in us.

One day, while Jesus was having dinner at someone's house, a woman came to Him and poured perfume on His feet. She was crying as she wiped His feet with her hair, showing how sorry she was for the wrong things she had done.

Read: Psalm 51:5, Luke 7:36-48, Psalm 51:10

Then Jesus said to her, "Your sins are forgiven."

Those few words of Jesus wiped out every wrong the woman had ever done. And that's what God promises to do for anyone who is sorry for their sin.

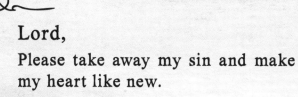

Lord,
Please take away my sin and make my heart like new.

Amen

God Gives Us What We Long For

Is there one thing you'd like more than anything else in the world? Perhaps it is for your family to be happy, or to have a loyal friend, or to sing well.

Your parents can give you *certain* things. By working hard, you could get something you really want. Yet, there are things that only God can give you.

There is a wonderful promise from God that says,

> Take delight in the LORD, and He will give you the desires of your heart.
>
> PSALM 37:4

More than anything, Hannah wanted a baby. Year after year, as she went to the temple with her husband, she was sad because she had no children. To make matters worse, she was teased because she couldn't be a mother.

But Hannah didn't give up hoping. One day, she decided to go to the temple. With tears rolling down her cheeks, she asked God for a son.

📖 Read: 1 Samuel 1

God heard Hannah's prayer, and it wasn't long before He let her have a son. And she called him Samuel, which means *God has heard*. Hannah's many years of sadness made this miracle all the more special.

Sometimes, God puts a longing in our hearts so that we will trust Him for what seems impossible. Then, as we pray in faith, a seed of hope grows in our hearts and we patiently wait to see what God will do.

Lord,

You can see deep down inside of me. You know my thoughts and the longing of my heart.

Amen

God Makes All Things Work for Our Good

Do you wonder why things go wrong; why bad things happen to people who are good?

Things started going wrong when people disobeyed God. Adam and Eve were given the freedom to think about things and to make choices. Sadly, they chose to do wrong. Their sin brought trouble into the world. It brought sadness, sickness and even death.

When we disobey, we always get into some kind of trouble. Sometimes we get hurt by bad choices that other people make. But God has an amazing way of letting something good come from the bad.

> God causes everything to work together for the good of those who love God and are called according to His purpose for them.
>
> ROMANS 8:28

Joseph had ten older brothers who were very jealous of him. One day they grabbed Joseph and threw him into a deep hole, where he would have died. But later, the brothers pulled him out

Read: Genesis 37:12-28, Genesis 50:20

and sold him to traders who were passing by. Joseph was taken to a faraway land where he had to work hard. But Joseph didn't mind and he always did his best, so his master liked and trusted him.

Then, one day, something bad happened. Joseph was sent to prison even though he had done nothing wrong. Yet Joseph was patient and believed that God would work out His perfect plan.

In time, God made good come from what Joseph's brothers had done to him. When there was no more food in Egypt, the king put Joseph in charge of a plan that saved the Egyptians, and his family from starving.

Lord,
I don't know Your plans for me, but I trust You to use even the bad things that happen for good.

Amen

God Helps Us Find Him

No one can see God because the light of His goodness is far too bright for us. So if we cannot see God, how can we look for Him and find Him?

God wants you to spend time with Him, just as you would spend time with a friend. Find a place where it is quiet. Let your thoughts talk to Him and let your heart feel His love. When you want to get close to God, He will come close to you. God promised,

> "When you look for Me, you will find Me.
> When you wholeheartedly seek Me."
>
> JEREMIAH 29:13

In his heart, Nicodemus wanted to know how he could find God. So he went to look for Jesus, for surely He would know. It was dark when Nicodemus came to Jesus with a longing in his heart, and many questions. Jesus helped him get straight to what he really wanted to know: how to find God.

"You need to be born again," Jesus told him. It was as simple as that.

And so, by going to Jesus, Nicodemus found God.

📖 Read: Exodus 33:20, James 4:8, John 3:1-16, Ezekiel 36:26

When you ask God to make you His child, you are born into His family. Although your body stays the same, your heart is made new. God puts a new spirit in you so that His Spirit can live in you. That is where you find God; living right inside you – closer than your closest friend.

Dear heavenly Father,
Please make my heart right so that I will love You and seek You with all my heart.
Amen

God Honors those Who Serve Him

To honor means to respect and to lift someone up. Honoring someone shows that person's worth. Jesus said,

> "My Father will honor the one who serves Me."
>
> JOHN 12:26

You may feel that you don't deserve to be honored. But it's not about how you see yourself, but how God sees you. You are valuable to God because Jesus gave His life for you. You are precious to God because He made you His child. You are beautiful to God because He lifted you from the dirt of sin and clothed you with His goodness.

Jesus needed a team of helpers who would watch Him, learn from Him, and do what He did. As He walked along the Sea of Galilee, He called the first two disciples. Peter and Andrew were ordinary fishermen, busy with their daily chores. When Jesus called them, they immediately left everything and followed Him. From that day on, they faithfully obeyed and served Jesus. And God honored them.

Read: Psalm 40:2, Isaiah 61:10, Matthew 4:18-20, Luke 14:11

When we serve God, He takes note. We serve Him by helping and encouraging others. We also serve by sharing what we have with others. When we give with a generous heart, and help with a humble heart, God will lift us up.

Lord,

I want to follow You as the disciples did. Help me to serve You faithfully.

Amen

God Rewards Us for the Good We Do

Have you recently been rewarded for being good? If so, well done!

In the Bible, there are many promises that God will reward us. This promise here is not a reward for *being* good, but for *doing* good. Paul said,

> "Remember that the Lord will reward each one of us for the good we do ..."
>
> **EPHESIANS 6:8**

It had not rained for a long time. The wheat crop had shriveled up and food was scarce. A poor, lonely woman was gathering sticks for a fire to bake her very last bread. Just then, the prophet Elijah came by. He first asked her for a little water. Then he asked for some food. Although the woman only had food for one more meal, she gave it to Elijah. God rewarded the woman's faith and kindness by doing a miracle.

From that day on, her jar of flour and her oil didn't get used up. She carried on using it day after day and there was always enough for another meal.

📖 Read: 1 Kings 17:7-16, Colossians 3:23-24, Matthew 10:42

When we are kind to others – even by giving someone a cup of water – God rewards us.

We may get some of our reward on earth, but another reward is waiting for us – our eternal reward stored up in heaven.

Lord,

I want to please You by being kind to others. Help me to think of ways that I can do good.

Amen

God Helps Us to Pray

Do you sometimes struggle to pray? Your heart wants to talk to God but you don't know what to say. Or sometimes it may feel as if your prayers aren't getting through to God.

God loves it when we talk to Him with simple words from the heart. The Holy Spirit takes the prayers we struggle to pray and adds His own heavenly words. He turns what we say into a beautiful prayer that becomes like a sweet smelling perfume to God.

> The Holy Spirit helps us in our weakness. For example, we don't know what God wants us to pray for. But the Holy Spirit prays for us with groanings that cannot be expressed in words.
>
> ROMANS 8:26

When you're not sure how to pray about something but you pray anyway, the Holy Spirit sees your faith and asks God to answer in the best possible way.

Cornelius believed in God. He was a good man who helped others and prayed often. But Cornelius didn't know Jesus, and he didn't know about being born again on the inside. Yet the Holy Spirit saw his heart and heard his prayers.

Read: Psalm 141:2, Acts 10:1-2, 24-45

And so God told Peter to go to Cornelius and tell him about Jesus. When Peter arrived, Cornelius and others listened to Peter's message. They all believed, and the Holy Spirit came to live in each of them.

Lord,
Thank You that my prayers are never wasted because You see my faith and You want to answer.

Amen

We Can Ask for Anything

Jesus has given us spiritual power to change the world for the better through our actions and through prayer. That's why He gave us this promise:

> "You may ask Me for anything in My name, and I will do it."
> JOHN 14:14

When Jesus was on earth, He saw the needs of people around Him, and He helped them. Then, when Jesus went back to heaven, He left us to carry on the work that He had started.

And so, when we see someone in need, we can ask Jesus to do for the person what He would have done if He were still on earth. That's what it means to pray in His name – to pray the kind of prayer Jesus would have prayed.

One day, Peter and John were going to the temple to pray. At the temple gate they saw a crippled man begging for money. Peter and John wanted to help the man, not just by giving him a few coins, but by doing something really amazing.

So Peter said to the man, "I don't have any money to give you, but what I do have I give to you. In the name of Jesus Christ,

get up and walk!" And immediately, the man jumped to his feet and started to walk.

When we pray the kind of prayer that pleases Jesus, we can end it with the words *"In Jesus' name."*

Heavenly Father,

I pray that You will ...... *(use your own words)*. I pray this in Jesus' name.

Amen

All power is given unto Me.

God Will Finish His Work in Us

Doesn't it feel frustrating when you're busy with something and you run out of time? Perhaps you're making something and you have to stop halfway.

You can be sure of this: your time on earth will not be up until God has finished His work in your life.

> God, who began the good work within you, will continue His work until it is finally finished.
>
> **PHILIPPIANS 1:6**

When God finished creating the world, He said, "It is very good!" Now, God is working on the inside of us – in our hearts. And when His work in us is done, He will also be able to say, "It is very good!" His work in our lives will be complete and perfect before our time is up.

Paul, who wrote this promise from God, was on His way to Damascus to kill and hurt those who believed in Jesus. He thought that they were wrong and wanted to stop them spreading the news about Jesus. But along the way, Jesus spoke from heaven, and everything changed for Paul.

Read: Genesis 1:31, Acts 9:1-9

From that day on, Paul faithfully served Jesus. Many years later, Paul wrote to his friend Timothy, saying, "You know me well. You know about my faith, my patience, my love, and my endurance."

Paul had not changed himself. God changed him! All *he* needed to do was be obedient and allow the Holy Spirit to change his heart. Instead of wanting to do wrong he now wanted to do what was good and right.

Lord,
You have started working in my heart, and one day Your perfect work in me will be done.
Amen

Jesus Is Getting a Place Ready for Us

The disciples of Jesus were worried and upset, so Jesus told them to trust Him and not be afraid. When we trust Jesus, we are also trusting God, and that means we have nothing to fear.

God is the One who created the universe and so it belongs to Him. That means that He is in charge! But there is more encouraging news.

While we are struggling with things here on earth, Jesus is busy in His Father's home, making a beautiful place for us to stay. Each day that goes by we get closer to the day when it will finally be finished.

Jesus said,

"When everything is ready, I will come and get you,
so that you will always be with Me where I am."

JOHN 14:3

Read: John 14:1-3, 1 Corinthians 2:9, Matthew 13:43, John 14:4-6

The place Jesus is preparing for us will be better than any place you can imagine. Never-ending goodness will shine like the sun, reflecting love and joy in colors we've never seen. Breathtaking music will float through heaven, celebrating God's kindness!

Each one will have a special place – a heavenly room – in God's beautiful home. But the best is that we'll be able to talk to Jesus as much as we want to because we will be right there with Him.

When Thomas asked Jesus about the way to heaven, Jesus said to him, "I am the Way." Only Jesus can forgive us and make us a child of God.

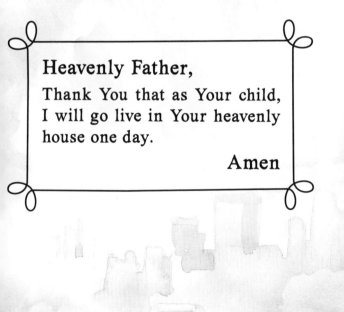

Heavenly Father,

Thank You that as Your child, I will go live in Your heavenly house one day.

Amen

Jesus Is Coming Back to Fetch Us

Before Jesus went up to heaven, He said that He would come back for us soon. This means that we should be ready for Him all the time with hearts that are pure and clean, like a bride on her wedding day.

On that great day, God's loud trumpet will sound and Jesus will come down from heaven. Those who have died believing in Christ will rise to meet Him first.

> "Then we who are living at that time will be gathered up along with them in the clouds to meet the Lord in the air. And so we will always be with the Lord."
>
> 1 THESSALONIANS 4:17

Imagine what it will be like to hear the trumpet of God and float up into the sky with all those who love Jesus. Think of what it will feel like to leave all your troubles behind and look into the smiling face of Jesus. When we are all with Him, He will take us to the beautiful place He's been preparing for us.

Read: John 14:3, Acts 1:10-11, 1 Corinthians 15:51-52, Revelation 22:12

Our bodies will be changed so that they can live forever. They will be absolutely perfect. We won't be able to sin anymore, and we will never feel pain or sadness again.

Jesus,

I long for the day when I will see You and be with You forever.

Amen

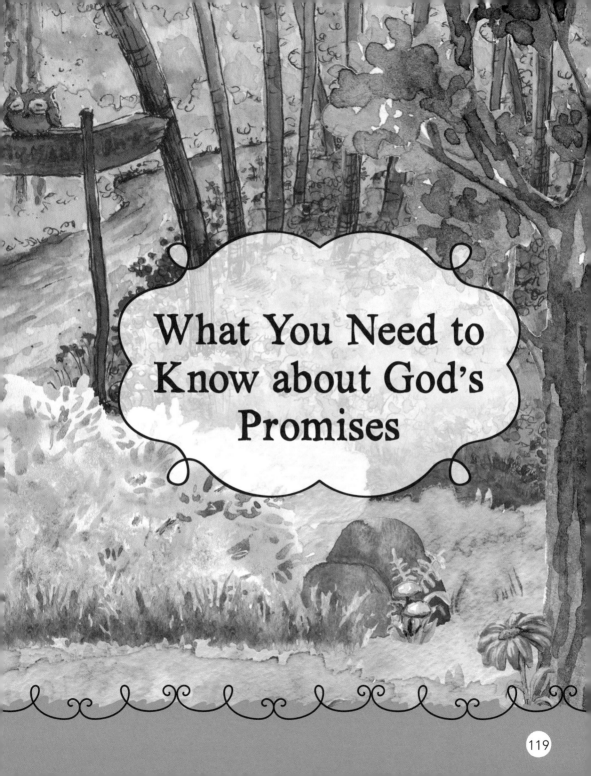

What You Need to Know about God's Promises

God's Promises, and Faith in Jesus

Many promises go unused because people don't believe that those promises are there for them.

Yet, in the Old Testament, the prophet Isaiah said that God would send someone to save, comfort and heal all people. Then God sent Jesus to earth to make this promise come true.

And so, because Jesus came, all of God's promises have been given to us.

> For no matter how many promises God
> has made, they are "Yes" in Christ.
> 2 Corinthians 1:20

There was an army officer whose servant had become very sick. The officer came to Jesus and said, "Lord, my servant is in a lot of pain and he might die."

Jesus was about to go heal the servant, but the officer said, "Lord, just stay here and say the word, and he will be healed."

Jesus said, "Go back home. What you believed will be done for you."

📖 Read: Isaiah 61:1-3, Luke 4:18-19, Matthew 8:5-13, Mark 6:5

In faith, the officer went home. When he got back, he found his servant completely well again. Sadly, the people in town where Jesus grew up didn't believe in Him. They didn't have faith, and so Jesus couldn't do the miracles God had promised.

Jesus,

I believe that You are the Son of God and that You make all Your promises happen.

Amen

Waiting for God's Promises

We can easily become discouraged when we have to wait for something that God promised, and nothing seems to happen. It is hard to just keep on hoping. Yet, hope helps our faith to grow, and our faith pleases God.

When we already have something, we no longer need to hope for it.

> But if we look forward to something
> we don't yet have, we must wait patiently
> and confidently.
>
> ROMANS 8:25

There was an old man in Jerusalem whose name was Simeon. He was a good and faithful man. The Holy Spirit had promised him in his heart that he would see Jesus the Savior before he died.

Perhaps he had waited for many, many years. Yet he didn't give up, trusting God for what He had promised.

Then one day, the Spirit told him to go to the temple. At that exact time, Joseph and Mary were there with their baby.

Simeon took baby Jesus in his arms and prayed, "Heavenly Lord, now that my eyes have seen the One who will save us, let me die peacefully just as You promised."

Just like Simeon, you will only see God's promise happen when the time is right, and it may even look different to what you expected. But you can be sure of this: when God speaks, it *will* happen.

Lord,
Help me to believe that Your promises are worth waiting for.

Amen

Reminding God of a Promise

The only thing God forgets is our sin – when we say sorry. He remembers everything else! So do we really need to remind God of His promises?

Perhaps it is not God who needs reminding, but us. When it seems as though nothing is happening, we want to make sure that the promise still stands. This is probably how the psalmist felt when he wrote,

> **Remember Your promise to me; it is my only hope.**
> **PSALM 119:49**

Talking to God about the promise gives us new hope. It reminds us of the first time God spoke the promise to our hearts.

Jacob had cheated his brother Esau. That made Esau so angry that Jacob had to run away from home. After many years, God told Jacob to go back home. Jacob was afraid that Esau would still be angry and perhaps even kill him. So he prayed, "Lord, remember Your promise to look after me, and to let my children become a great nation."

Read: Psalm 105:8, Genesis 32:9-12

God heard Jacob's prayer and did what he had promised. Esau forgave Jacob, and as the years went by, Jacob's sons became the nation of Israel.

God loves it when we pray His promises back to Him. He is honored by our faith when we hold on to a promise He has made.

Lord,

I will not forget Your promises because they give me hope.

Amen

Thanking God for a Promise

Do you say thank you for a gift even before you've unwrapped it?

Promises are like word gifts. God gives us a special promise just when we need it.

At first, we may not know what the gift looks like, yet we can still say thank you. By thanking God, we are showing that we trust Him to make the promise come true in the right way and at the right time.

God told the Israelites that He would lead them safely out of Egypt to the Promised Land. When things went well, they trusted God; like when He opened up the Red Sea so they could walk through on dry land.

> **Then they believed His promises
> and sang His praise.**
>
> **PSALM 106:12**

Read: Psalm 106:1-13, Numbers 14:2, Philippians 4:6

While the Israelites trusted God, they were happy and sang songs of praise to Him. With great excitement they looked forward to their new land.

But when things didn't go their way, they grumbled and complained, and so they made themselves miserable.

If you want to stay happy, praise God for who He is and thank Him for what He has done. This will please your heavenly Father.

Dear Lord,
I praise You for Your love, and the power You have to make all Your promises come true.

Amen